Put Beginning Readers on the Right Track with
ALL ABOARD READING™

The All Aboard Reading series is especially designed for beginning readers. Written by noted authors and illustrated in full color, these are books that children really want to read—books to excite their imagination, expand their interests, make them laugh, and support their feelings. With fiction and nonfiction stories that are high interest and curriculum-related, All Aboard Reading books offer something for every young reader. And with four different reading levels, the All Aboard Reading series lets you choose which books are most appropriate for your children and their growing abilities.

Picture Readers
Picture Readers have super-simple texts, with many nouns appearing as rebus pictures. At the end of each book are 24 flash cards—on one side is a rebus picture; on the other side is the written-out word.

Station Stop 1
Station Stop 1 books are best for children who have just begun to read. Simple words and big type make these early reading experiences more comfortable. Picture clues help children to figure out the words on the page. Lots of repetition throughout the text helps children to predict the next word or phrase—an essential step in developing word recognition.

Station Stop 2
Station Stop 2 books are written specifically for children who are reading with help. Short sentences make it easier for early readers to understand what they are reading. Simple plots and simple dialogue help children with reading comprehension.

Station Stop 3
Station Stop 3 books are perfect for children who are reading alone. With longer text and harder words, these books appeal to children who have mastered basic reading skills. More complex stories captivate children who are ready for more challenging books.

In addition to All Aboard Reading books, look for All Aboard Math Readers™ (fiction stories that teach math concepts children are learning in school); All Aboard Science Readers™ (nonfiction books that explore the most fascinating science topics in age-appropriate language); All Aboard Poetry Readers™ (funny, rhyming poems for readers of all levels); and All Aboard Mystery Readers™ (puzzling tales where children piece together evidence with the characters).

All Aboard for happy reading!

For Sissy—S.S.

To my gorgeous children Henry and Charlotte—P.B.

GROSSET & DUNLAP
Published by the Penguin Group
Penguin Group (USA) Inc., 375 Hudson Street, New York, New York 10014, USA
Penguin Group (Canada), 90 Eglinton Avenue East, Suite 700,
Toronto, Ontario M4P 2Y3, Canada (a division of Pearson Penguin Canada Inc.)
Penguin Books Ltd., 80 Strand, London WC2R 0RL, England
Penguin Group Ireland, 25 St. Stephen's Green, Dublin 2, Ireland
(a division of Penguin Books Ltd.)
Penguin Group (Australia), 250 Camberwell Road, Camberwell, Victoria 3124, Australia
(a division of Pearson Australia Group Pty. Ltd.)
Penguin Books India Pvt. Ltd., 11 Community Centre, Panchsheel Park,
New Delhi—110 017, India
Penguin Group (NZ), 67 Apollo Drive, Rosedale, North Shore 0632, New Zealand
(a division of Pearson New Zealand Ltd.)
Penguin Books (South Africa) (Pty.) Ltd., 24 Sturdee Avenue, Rosebank,
Johannesburg 2196, South Africa

Penguin Books Ltd., Registered Offices:
80 Strand, London WC2R 0RL, England

Text copyright © 2008 by Samantha Brooke. Illustrations copyright © 2008 by Peter Bull Art
Studio. All rights reserved. Published by Grosset & Dunlap, a division of Penguin Young Readers
Group, 345 Hudson Street, New York, New York 10014. ALL ABOARD SCIENCE READER
and GROSSET & DUNLAP are trademarks of Penguin Group (USA) Inc. Printed in the U.S.A.

Library of Congress Cataloging-in-Publication Data

Brooke, Samantha.
Coral reefs : in danger / by Samantha Brooke ; illustrated by Peter Bull.
p. cm.
ISBN 978-0-448-44872-5 (pbk.)
1. Coral reef ecology--Juvenile literature. 2. Coral reefs and islands--Juvenile literature. I.
Bull, Peter, 1960- ill. II. Title.
QH541.5.C7B755 2008
578.77'89--dc22
2007042328

ISBN 978-0-448-44872-5   10 9 8 7 6 5 4 3 2 1

Coral Reefs
In Danger

By Samantha Brooke
Illustrated by Peter Bull

Grosset & Dunlap

It is morning.

The sun rises

over the ocean.

Something is poking

out of the water.

It looks like a tree branch.

But it is not a tree branch.

It is coral.

Below the waves

is a busy world—

the world of a coral reef.

A coral reef is home

to many creatures.

Thousands of different small fish

live here.

So do sharks, eels, and octopuses.

Whales and sea turtles

also come to visit.

Coral reefs grow in

warm, salty water.

On this map

coral reefs are in red.

Most are near the equator

in shallow water.

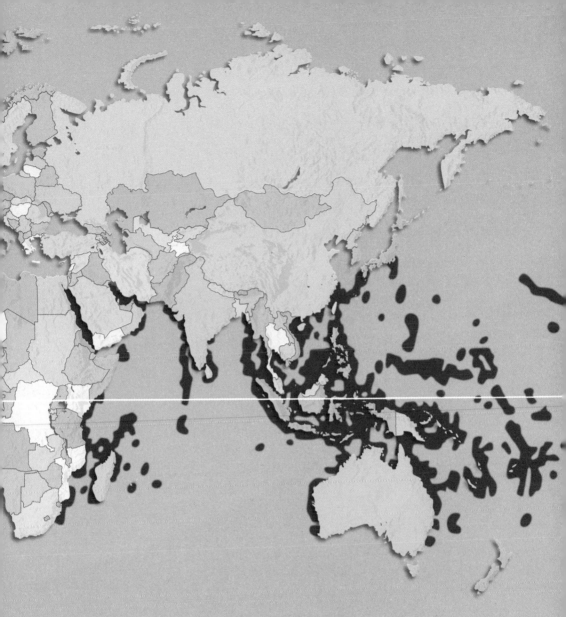

That's because a coral reef

needs lots of sunlight.

Deep water is too dark

and cold for most forms of coral.

Great Barrier Reef

Australia

The largest reef is
off the coast of Australia.
The Great Barrier Reef
stretches for over 1,250 miles.
Astronauts can see it
from space!

But if coral isn't a rock,

what exactly is it?

Coral is an animal.

The hard outside

is the skeleton.

Inside is the animal.

Lobsters and crabs also have

skeletons on the outside.

A coral reef starts

with one small polyp.

(You say polyp like this: POL-up.)

It attaches itself to a rock.

The polyp is shaped like a tube.

Its mouth is at the top.

Around the mouth are tiny tentacles

that help catch food.

Over and over again

a polyp sprouts new polyps.

It is like a trec

with new branches.

Coral grows very slowly.

And it always stays

in the same place.

A group of the same polyps

is called a colony.

A colony can grow to be

as big as a house.

It can live for hundreds of years.

Not all coral colonies look the same.

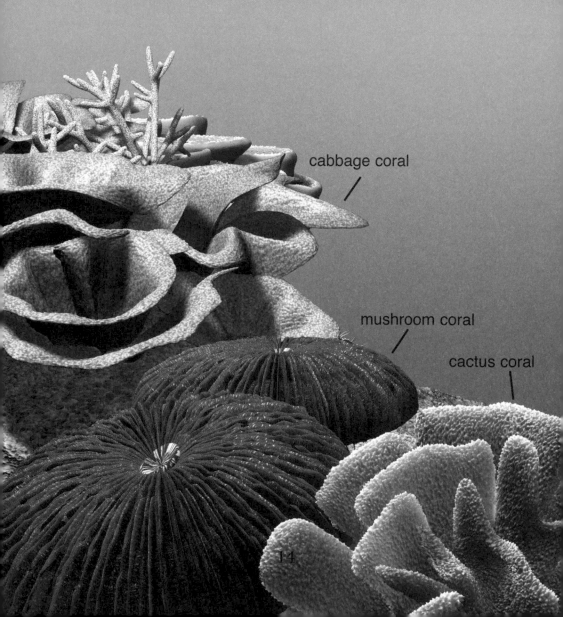

cabbage coral

mushroom coral

cactus coral

14

Staghorn coral
looks like deer antlers.
Mushroom coral
looks like the underside
of a mushroom.

finger coral

brain coral

Daytime is the best time
to visit a coral reef.
That's when colorful fish
are out and about.

There are thousands
of different fish in a reef.

At night,

colorful fish are in danger.

Sharks, eels, rays, and octopuses

come hunting for food.

Many fish hide deep in the reef.

Others swim to deeper water.

That doesn't stop sharks from hunting.

Sharks use their sense of smell
to find food.
But this white-tipped reef shark
swims right by a parrot fish.
Why?
The parrot fish has wrapped itself
in a sticky bubble.
The shark cannot smell it.

In the dark,

an octopus uses

its eight arms to feel for food.

It has grabbed a crab.

But moray eels are also out at night.

And they like to eat octopus!

The eel attacks.

It bites the octopus on one arm.

But the octopus can break off

its own arm!

Now it is free.

It squirts out a cloud of dark ink.

This is its chance to escape.

Whoooosh! Off it goes!

At night, coral finds food.

Out come its tentacles.

The tentacles have

poison stingers.

Back and forth

they wave in the water.

They trap tiny plants and animals

floating by.

Then the sun rises.

The coral tentacles

go back inside the polyp.

The colorful fish come out of hiding.

Another day begins in the life of the reef.

Coral reefs have existed

for millions of years.

They were around

even before the dinosaurs.

But they are more than just

a beautiful home

for fish and plants.

Reefs help protect the shore

from storms.

They provide food and medicines.

But coral reefs are in danger!

And the enemy is us.

Boom!

Sometimes fishermen use dynamite
to kill many fish at once.
The blast can destroy
a coral reef.

Pollution on shore

can harm coral reefs

and the fish who live there.

Fertilizers help crops grow.

But fertilizers can seep

into the ground

and wash out to sea.

They, too, harm coral reefs.

But perhaps

the greatest danger to reefs

is global warming.

Global warming means

that the average temperature

of the entire Earth is increasing.

Have you heard
of greenhouse gases?
They are natural gases
in the atmosphere.
They form a layer
around our planet.
Greenhouse gasses help keep our planet
nice and warm.

Just like the glass walls of a greenhouse,
gases like carbon dioxide
hold in heat from the sun.
But people have been adding
more and more of these gases
to the atmosphere.

How?

We release these gases

when we drive cars . . .

when we use electricity,

and when we heat or cool our homes.

The layer of greenhouse gases

has become too thick.

Too much heat is trapped

in the atmosphere.

This means the weather is warmer

in many parts of our planet.

But what does global warming

have to do with coral reefs?

When the ocean

is even a little bit too warm,

coral may bleach.

It turns ghostly gray or white.

Bleaching can be a sign that

the coral is about to die.

Scientists worry about

the coral reefs.

The green areas show
coral reefs that are in danger.
Up to one-third of the world's coral reefs
have already died.

It is not too late

to save coral reefs.

It is not too late

to stop global warming.

Here are some things

you can do to help.

Ask your family to walk or ride bikes

to places close by.

Try to use less electricity.

Remember to turn off lights.

In winter,

use less fuel

to heat your home.

Wear a sweater indoors.

In summer,
use less air-conditioning.
Open a window
for a cool breeze.

Plant a tree!

Trees remove carbon dioxide
from the air.

(Remember, carbon dioxide is one of
the major greenhouse gases.)

Tree roots also hold on to soil.

They stop too much sediment

from getting into the ocean.

Sediment makes the water

too cloudy for coral to grow.

Coral reefs are

truly one of the world's

natural wonders.

We must do our part

to make sure that coral reefs

will be around

for millions of years to come.